Advance Praise for

Extraordinary poetry -- pure bhakti!

Roger Woolger, world-renowned Jungian analyst, past-life healer and author of numerous books including *The Goddess Within*.

+++

This collection of devotional poems, a rarity in today's world, will awaken the heart of love within any reader whatever their spiritual tradition. Lawrence Edwards, a long time devotee of the Devi (the archetypal feminine that exists within all), has had the blessings of some of the leading Masters of our time. As these ecstatic poems reveal, he provides a shining example of the spiritual life fully lived, able to embrace with eloquence all of life's extremes from suffering to bliss. These poems are in the tradition of the great ecstatic poets such as Rumi, Kabir, Hafiz and others. They transport the reader beyond this world of duality into unconditioned Oneness, a rare gift indeed!

Most of the poems came to Kalidas during meditation by "the Divine's power of Grace." Others were born amidst the challenges of daily life. The sign of a wise teacher, he doesn't separate the inner, devotional life from the world's suffering, but rather weaves them together masterfully. These poems radiate a passionate, timeless, love-saturated intensity and will touch your heart in unimaginable ways.

Olivia Ames Hoblitzelle, author of
Ten Thousand Joys & Ten Thousand Sorrows:
A Couple's Journey Through Alzheimer's.
Named Best Buddhist Writer, 2009
TenThousandJoysAndSorrows.com

Here, gathered over many years of quest and deep experience, is a beautiful symposium of devotional poems to awaken the mind and rejoice the heart. The introduction is a powerful call to the incandescent reality of inner experience. Here are poems to savor, to guide, to bring tears and, above all, to dissolve the veil that lies between us and the Divine Presence who tells us that we live within Her Being and Her Love.

Anne Baring, British Jungian analyst and author of *One Work: A Journey Toward The Self* and co-author with Andrew Harvey of *The Mystic Vision* and *The Divine Feminine.* AnneBaring.com

+++

The poignant imagery and keen spiritual insights I found in Kali's Bazaar's delighted me. But what moved me even more was that they revealed Lawrence – whose vast knowledge and rare understanding of Eastern traditions have long marked as a man of profound intellect – to be a man of even deeper heart....

Teri Degler, author of *The Divine Feminine Fire* and *The Fiery Muse: Creativity and the Spiritual Quest,* and international workshop leader on the Divine Feminine. TeriDegler.com

Those on a sacred path will recognize that Kalidas (Lawrence Edwards) has made an authentic life journey and, through his poetry, is sharing his piercing insights and exalted states. His relationship to the Mother allows us to hear her voice in every sound, to see her magnificence in every sight, to feel her fiercely loving caress in every touch, and to sense the rhythm of her beating heart in our soul. Reading these poems transports and transforms the reader through delight and deep satisfaction.

> Martin Lowenthal, Psychologist, Tibetan Buddhist, Founder of the Dedicated Life Institute and author of several books, including *Alchemy of the Soul* and *Buddha and the Art of Intimacy*.
> Dli.org

+++

In this collection, Kalidas (servant of Kali) offers us the distillation of a lifetime of spiritual seeking and devotion. Each poem glows with the iridescent spark of that sacred essence left in the alchemist's dish when all the dross has been sifted away. Yeats used the phrase "when naked to naked goes" to describe such moments, when the unadorned soul unites with the Beloved in shameless adoration. These poems allow us to observe at close hand this profound process by which the mundane substance of the material self is transmuted into the clarity of the refined being, the gold of pure spirit.

Continued, next page.

For years living a monk's life in India, later an accomplished Jungian therapist, workshop leader, and meditation master, Kalidas (Lawrence Edwards, Ph.D.) now devotes much of his time to helping others on the path, particularly those undergoing unexpected Kundalini awakening. This is the gift he returns to the world, precious goods recovered from a lifetime voyage into the authentic self.

Dorothy Walters, Ph.D., poet and author of
numerous works including *Unmasking the Rose, A Record of a Kundalini Initiation* and *Marrow of Flame: Poems of the Spiritual Journey.*
KundaliniSplendor.Blogspot.com

++

With great humility (a sign of an authentic teacher) Lawrence Edwards reveals to us his spiritual inner life so we can accept our own inner experiences instead of thinking something might be terribly wrong.

As we read these devotional poems aloud to each other we discovered - not new landscapes but the same landscapes with new eyes. This beautiful writing reminded us that Spirit is in everything including our relationships. Kali's Bazaar is definitely a gift of grace for anyone, including couples to share.

Charles L. Whitfield MD,
author of *Choosing God* and
Teachers of God

Barbara Harris Whitfield,
author of *Spiritual Awakenings* and
The Natural Soul
Barbara-Whitfield.Blogspot.com.com

Kali's Bazaar

Penned by
Kalidas

Gifts of Devotion to the Divine,
Buddhist Wisdom, and Kundalini Yoga Tantra

Lawrence Edwards, PhD

ᴍᴴP
muse house press

ꟽꞪP
muse house press

ISBN: 978-1-935827-09-2

Trade Paperback
Copyright ©2011 Lawrence Edwards
All Rights Reserved

First Edition

Find us on the Internet at:
www.MuseHousePress.com

Muse House Press and the MHP Logo
are imprints of Muse House Press.
The red triangle and Ouroboros logo
is a Trademark of Lawrence Edwards.

Cover design and interior composition by:
Donald Brennan / Muse House Press
Illustrations by Molly Edwards

Use and permission requests should be addressed to
info@thesoulsjourney.com or in writing to:
Lawrence Edwards
PO Box 541166
Cincinnati, OH 45254

www.TheSoulsJourney.com

Printed in the United States of America

Kali's Bazaar

Penned by
Kalidas

Table of Contents

More books from Lawrence Edwards, PhD and
Muse House Press authors

Introduction

Dearest Reader,

These poems were penned as accurately as possible as they appeared during meditative states which were often suffused with the gifts of unimaginably sublime ecstasy and overwhelming Love. (Such living meditative states aren't limited to sitting in a classic posture or specified time of practice.) Gathered along the path of devotion, the poems are gifts of grace, of Love, to be passed on to others. The path of Love, the path of devotion - bhakti yoga in the yogic tradition - fully engages the heart, mind, body and spirit of the seeker. The highest knowing is experienced through loving merger with the Infinite and the divine play of Lover and Beloved. I didn't begin my spiritual pursuits this way. I started out as an intellectual, seeking with the mind, studying Buddhism, Vedanta and yoga; doing practices of watching the breath, meditating with clarity, focus and energy, seeking an abstract Witness Consciousness, Buddha Mind, Transcendent Infinitude. I was blind to love and devotion. I didn't think of the heart. I didn't engage the heart or even want to remember it. In fact, I found the heart to be a problem. Feelings were obstacles to be subdued, mere mud that once stirred had to be allowed to settle before the clarity and light of the mind could be regained. Of course I didn't know *That* which illumines even the darkness and density of the mind.

Fortunately, the Heart of hearts has never forgotten us, regardless of how long we may have turned away from Her. One of the poems in this collection ends with "Choose Love/For Love has already chosen you." Perhaps that's all that really needs to be said about the great paths to knowing and living the highest truth. Though I can say that now, from where I sit now, where I started from decades ago was very different. I grew up in an average suburb of New York City, on Long Island, and rebelling all the way, went through a disengaged confirmation process in the Methodist Church. But there was within me a very alive longing to know what lies beyond the ordinary mind and the ordinary things that occupy us all. I wrote more about this in my book *The Soul's Journey: Guidance From The Divine Within* and won't go into that here. Suffice it to say that I was blessed with heart and mind opening experiences of the Infinite One clothed in exquisite archetypal forms divine, as well as experiences of dissolution into formlessness which forever altered my view of the entire world and every being within it.

Early in my 20's when some of these types of experiences were first coming to me in meditation I was moved by them to find a way to live a life purely and solely dedicated to serving the Divine. At the time my teacher was a monk, a swami, a total renunciate in the Vedic tradition, so I prepared to leave my career, fiancé, and family to go to India to follow in that tradition. My father asked me to speak with my uncle, a retired Methodist minister, Rev. Dr. Norman O. Edwards. He was the only minister who was what I called "juicy." God was a living presence to him and his preaching was the only preaching I had ever heard that felt alive. We spoke and at the end he said he wished I had found what I was seeking in the church, but he was happy for me that I had found it at all.

Swami Muktananda, my beloved teacher until he shed that form in 1982, had the wisdom to open the doors of my heart and mind further. Rather than taking me and forming a likeness of himself as so many "gurus" do, this master guided me in becoming a better knower and servant of the Divine within us all. He eventually sent me back into the world with a view that embraced the whole universe as the body of the Divine. I will never be able to express my gratitude for what he and other teachers have given me. The teachings and empowerments I've received from His Holiness the Dalai Lama, His Eminence Tulku Tsewang Seetar Rinpoche and his brother Lama Pema Tenzin, Chogyam Trungpa Rinpoche, one of my earliest teachers, and numerous others, have remade this one into a better implement to be held and used by my Devi.

When I use the word "Devi" I mean the feminine face of the Infinite One which is the facet of the Divine that has been central to grace unfolding in my life. Love and devotion are the feeling connections that relate us, me, to that One and to that One in all Her forms. These sublime feelings are part of the archetypal feminine present in all of us. Without them we feel disconnected, abstracted, alienated, and unrelated. Thus true and full knowing of the Ineffable are impossible.

Until these feelings and ways of knowing through Love, union and merger - the way of the heart - were given to me through the Divine's power of Grace, I suffered the hubris of thinking the mind could expand to grasp in some super inflated way *That* which is forever beyond the mind. The power of Grace so humbles the mind that in the end, like Arjuna in the Bhagavad Gita, it finally surrenders and asks of the Infinite to simply do Thy bidding.

Like countless other seekers, early on I began experiencing the Divine in feminine forms - archetypal, living, moving, speaking forms of the Goddess began appearing in meditation. Many I had never seen or heard of before and I had to research things about them to discover who they were. Kundalini, the black Madonna, Inanna, Kwan Yin, Tara, Saraswati, and on and on until Kali, the great mysterious black form of the Goddess began appearing. Fortunately my teachers, the practices and teachings, including my Jungian training, have allowed this ego mind, this conventional self, to remain intact while encountering these powerful living forms of the Divine that we can all have access to.

Kali is known as the Great Mother, the one who creates all the forms that appear in the universe and withdraws them all back into Herself. She is a fierce protector of true seekers. Creator and Destroyer, Lover and Beloved, She is all that is. When I first encountered Her decades ago in meditation I was completely overwhelmed and I was afraid to even contemplate the experience for many months. I literally wondered how a suburban New Yorker could possibly be having mind blowing experiences of the Hindu Goddess Maha Kali! Decades later it didn't surprise me that as She appeared in the form of Tara telling me to learn of Her in those forms, suddenly I was introduced to a great master of the Tibetan Buddhist Tara tradition visiting from his monastery in Bhutan, His Eminence Tsewang Seetar Rinpoche. Nothing is impossible for Her!

There are many forces at work in our psyches that move in the depths beyond the superficial, ordinary mind with which we are so identified. Fortunately these deeper forces, including the center, the Self, what C. G. Jung referred to as the transcendent integrative function, can digest experiences and empower the poor ego mind to come to terms with these huge powers, including the archetypal projections of Kali, while continuing to function and eventually to wake up! Wake up to all that exists beyond the ordinary mind, wake up to every being's ephemeral existence as a cell within the infinite body of the Divine, wake up to our innate power to know unfathomable, all-embracing Love. This is the true home we long for, the true embrace of the Lover we ache for, the only true knowing that brings complete peace to the mind.

The Source, the power and wisdom of Love, which attempts to push its way into this world through the words of these poems reveal Her gifts. Please look beyond the words, please feel beyond the words, please hear beyond the words for what is truly being offered by Her, and imperfectly conveyed by this scribe.

I pray that you fully receive all that She has to give.

In Her service,
Kalidas

Dear Mind,
you are the Creator's
organ of creation.
I fashioned you out of
My own substance and
being,
My sublime instrument
for shaping the
formlessness
of our own essence.

You're so accustomed
to becoming,
My dear servant,
so eager to fulfill
My every urge
to manifest our infinite
play of forms.

My dear One,
you've been at this
so long you're suffering
from becoming
the becomer!

Even when you hear
of true freedom,
of unbreakable union,

of eternal joy,
you faithfully try to
become that,
even willing to spend
lifetimes earnestly
engaged in various
contorted pursuits,
trying to become what
We already are.

This becoming has
become an addiction!

But don't worry!
You don't need 12 steps,
you don't even need
one step.
There's no distance to
traverse.
And, as hard as this is for
you to imagine,
there really isn't anything
for you to become.

So please relax and let go.
We're getting a cramp
in our hand!

There is but one
blasphemy,
one sin,
to mistake the part
for the whole.

Doorways are such small portals
we leave our vastness outside
whenever we pass through one.

When you entered this world,
you left your Infinitude
on the other side of the womb.

Searching and yearning,
forever restless,
driven by incompleteness,
you united once again with peace
on the other side of the tomb.

Why wait?
Die while living,
die while meditating,
and know you can never
be severed from your
Boundless, ecstatic nature!

Haven't You heard?

O Seeker!
You wish to build a mansion of happiness
in which to dwell for all your days,
Upon what foundation will you raise your mansion?

You wish to build a palace of peace,
a place of refuge for all times,
Upon what foundation will your palace rest?

You wish to build a temple of love
with fountains of devotion
to cleanse you of all impurities,
Upon what foundation will your temple find steady support?

You've built castles of joy
on the shifting sands of the senses,
How long have they stood?

You've sculpted tranquil inner landscapes
from personal accomplishments and professional degrees,
Can they withstand the ravages of time and the scorn of others?

You've searched through a desert of relationships
for the site of love's shrine, the wellspring of devotion.
What have you found but tear drops and dust?

Your endeavors have amounted to naught.
You cannot create the Eternal,
only the ignorant and the proud try.
Through the Grace of the Master know the Truth.

O Seeker!
With reverence listen to the Self of all:
My dear one, haven't you heard?
The doors to the mansion of happiness
have been thrown open to welcome you!
Leave behind the poverty of the five petty realms,

Follow the ecstatic ones who have crossed the bridge of grace
to the abode of the ever blissful Self!
Turn within and discover the divine mansion of the Infinite!

Innumerable rooms of pure joy await you!
My dear one, haven't you heard?

The palace of peace is before you -- just the other side of time.
Leave behind the delusion of doing and not doing,
Follow the ecstatic ones who have crossed the bridge of grace
and found repose on the throne of contentment.
Turn within and discover the palace of the Self!
You are the rightful Lord of the realm of Eternity!
Sit on your throne and enjoy unwavering peace.

My dear one, don't you remember?
Love's shrine has always been your true home.
Leave behind the wants and needs of mind and body.
Follow the ecstatic ones who have crossed the bridge of grace
never more to return.

Enter the Temple of Love
and discover where Lover and Beloved have gone.

Turn within,
dance along the path of love shown by the Master.
It will take you directly to the abode of God.

In the cloud
    raindrops swirl,
In the mind
    thoughts.
Ha! There is no
    rainmaker!

Love and longing
for the Divine,
These are Her forms
most sublime!

A faint glow in the Eastern sky
A blush on the face of the Divine
like my Devi smiling at me
in Love's embrace.

My Dear One,

Look into the mirror of a loving heart and
    behold your Self.

Sit with your children in the space of love,
    look into their eyes and behold your Self.

Rest in the place of inner stillness and spaciousness,
    look around and behold your Self.

Though you've put on the cloaks of anger,
    impatience, hunger and disease,
these can never be more than outer coverings.

Your beauty has been hidden at times,
    but never sullied.

The mountain stands steady in its grandeur
rising from the mists of the lowlands,
summit shrouded in clouds of unknowing.
A hidden path winds it way up from the jungle,
     lost to all but one in love.
Blessed by the Devi,
she endured the hardships,
followed her inspiration
and entered the cave of the heart of the mountain.
Her sanctuary found
she shed the coarse garments of the world
and surrendered to the quiet ecstasy of utter stillness
deep within her mountain,
unaware that at that moment,
a thousand birds rose from the mountainside,
taking flight in joy!

When soot blackens
the chimney of a lamp,
who would waste time yelling
at the flame for not shining
brightly enough?

Patiently clean the impurities from the glass of
    your mind,
the brilliance and beauty of your true nature
will illumine all around you
with the light of Love.

Sri Kundalini Shakti Mahadevi!

You delight in appearing clothed in many dresses.
Your lovers perceive your presence behind all your disguises.
You are the Amitabha, Prajnaparamitahrdayam,
Avalokiteshwara and Her boundless compassion
        for the Buddhists,
The Holy Spirit, Sophia and Mary
        for the followers of Christ,
And the wine of ecstasy drunk
        by the Sufis.
You are the power in the yogi's diverse practices,
        the devotion of bhaktas,
The sword of discrimination and
        the pure knowledge of Vedantins.
Your are the Shekhinah and her Source
        for the Kabbalists,
And the Tao
        of the Taoists.
Whatever our path to God, the power that carries us forward
        and the Illumination attained
Are alluring forms taken by you to draw us to
        the realization of the One.
Seeker, choose a path that most suits your temperament
        and give it your full attention.

Enjoy all the ways the Mother

Will reveal Herself and Her Spouse
        To you
                along
                        the way.

23

In the pre-dawn hours
a lush scent of the Divine
covers me in a blanket of grace.
Love's blessings quiet my soul
and the countenance of my Beloved
     fills my sight.
Time dissolves into eternity.

My heart is a temple
Where my Beloved is worshipped
With great respect and love.

My heart is a spacious refuge
Where I rest contented with
My Beloved.

My heart is a hall of mirrors
Constantly reflecting
My Beloved's beauty.

My heart is your home,
O My Beloved Devi.

Where have you gone my Beloved?
Please don't torture your faithful servant!
In a moment of weakness my gaze turned away,
    when I looked back you had vanished.
What am I to do?
The world is empty without *you*,
    my body a shell without my Beloved.
Bestow your grace my sweet Devi,
    reveal Yourself within and without!
I can barely breathe any longer.
Come quickly my Love, come quickly!
Or explain to my family why I have died.

The Flames of Love

Let the flames of Love cleanse you
    of all clinging to illusion.
Let Love illumine the Truth.

Love is the most precious gift.
Love is the most sublime path.
Love is the most profound meditation.
Love is the highest attainment.

In Love – the fullness of compassion.
In Love – timeless patience.
In Love – unbounded awareness.
In Love – all is illuminated.
In Love – vast spaciousness.
In Love – form and emptiness embrace.
In Love – I and Thou disappear.
In Love –

One Heart

The weary soul
Tired from the weight of masks
Worn through the day
To fend off assaults
From other weary souls
Too tired to remember why they are here
Too tired to remember what they know
Too tired to see beyond the pain.

All he seeks is to shed the masks,
the armor,
the clothes of the day.
A bottle of wine
and all falls away.
A respite found in the depths of sleep
lasts too briefly.
The body awakens,
puts on the masks,
puts on the clothes,
puts on the dense cloaks,
burying the light ever deeper.
His bright armor is no substitute.
Bracing himself he returns to the world
unprepared for the encounter,
unprepared for the sudden remembering,
unprepared for the Beloved,
stripping away layer after layer 'til
the naked heart quivers in Love,
the soul breathes as if for the first time,
breathes in the Beloved,
merges in the Beloved,
finally comes to rest in the Beloved,
inhaled by Her.
Not even a shadow of wanting
can slip within the embrace of the Beloved.
Do you remember?

Do you remember wanting to breathe,
to breathe like that?
One Breath
One Heart
Hafiz knew what it is to be the Heart.
Clothes no longer fit.
Masks keep falling off
or sit ridiculously askew.
Armor hurts.
He wanders the world
crying out the name of his Beloved
seeking the nectar of Love,
knowing nothing else will satisfy his thirst,
lost in a world desperately believing
it can wear the perfect mask
and hide behind the perfect shield
and fill the inner void
by consuming everything in sight.
Clothed in ignorance the world
destroys itself.
Better to live with the pain of
longing for the Beloved -
Her touch
Her breath
Her taste
Her scent
Her all-embracing Love,
than to be lost again in such delusion.
Your soul knows the Truth of who you are
and what you long for.
Never be content with shadows.

Sullen gray skies and cold winter rain
ice and snow reluctantly melt,
running off hard, frozen ground
still gripped by winter.
How long before all
this too will melt
away.

Overheard at sesshin:
"O, you broke my samadhi with all your noise!"
Very funny!
Who is there to own this samadhi?
What is this that breaks?
Sleep can be broken.
Dreams can be broken.
Ordinary wakefulness can be broken.
Delusions can be broken.
Relationships can be broken.
Attachments can be broken.
I can be broken.

Who asks of enlightenment?
Who?
Who answers?
Who?
The one who would like to answer,
will never know.

Nirvana simply is.
Samadhi simply is.
Simply Be
Empty
Silent
Spacious
Free.

Take a sword and slash the air before you.
Show me the seam you've created.
Samadhi is more seamless than air,
more boundless than space,
embracing all
as sweet Tara's Love.
Dissolve your "I" in Her.
She'll give you what you seek.

Possessed

My Devi took possession
    of my heart.
She knew she wanted me
    body and soul.
She played the wounded doe,
    opening the heart's door of compassion,
She slipped inside.
Now who is Lover and who is Beloved?

This Mind Like a Firefly

This mind, like a firefly, flashes into existence,
Just to call lovers of the Dark One!
Having been summoned into my beloved Kali,
Her Blackness so mystical, so absorbing,
the mind disappears in Her like a candle dropping
into the midnight ocean,
    even the cry of ecstasy is lost in Her depths!
Yet those who gaze into Her unfathomable Void
    take on a glow that those with sight can see!
How sublime to reflect Her Dark Light!
How sublime to share Her grace-filled gifts!
Extinguish yourself in Her this very instant!
She has waited so long, so patiently
    to embrace you — Her Beloved.

Wounds

Some speak of wounds.
Wounds are for the living.
True Love seeks annihilation.
The wounded one dies to Love.
Christ knew.
Kabir knew.
Hafiz knew.
Where there were two
Now there's only One.

The Dark

Into the Dark,
Her Dark,
mind silenced effortlessly,
its dancing little flame
blown out by Her breath,
drowned in Her Love.

We expend so much energy in petty pursuits,
chasing our tails, conflicted over this or that desire
with this or that person or group.......
dancing our petty dance on an illusory cloud
we think is solid ground,
    suspended over an ocean - an infinite ocean
of Love,
of Compassion,
of Emptiness!
In an instant you can let go of the illusion.
Drop through the cloud,
Splash!
You're in the Ocean!
You are free!
Right now!

Jai Kali Ma!
What mind can possibly approach you,
Much less grasp you, my beloved Kali!
This ordinary mind longs for you to be simple,
predictable, easily appreciated, a sweet divinity,
a demure goddess, lovely to look at, engendering kindness.
Instead you parade forth in gruesome reality,
unabashed, you unleash your limitless creative power,
thrilling the mind and body
    with overwhelming sensual delights,
propelling the spirit into awe-inspiring
    transcendent domains and
crushing us all in your jaws of time, decay and suffering.

You gave birth to Ignorance and her offspring,
"lacking this" and "wanting that" populate the universe.
Is there nothing you don't delight in creating?
How is this poor mind ever going to truly worship you?
I set out to circumambulate your divine form,
    to do puja to you,
but lifetimes of effort have left me gasping,
seeing your infinitude spread out in all directions,
    my mind and heart quiver
with fear and adoration, longing for annihilation in you,
    my beloved.

You demand full and total sacrifice,
not flower garlands and coins tossed at a statue,
not merely lighting candles and prostrating piously,
not sitting still as a corpse lost in the illusion
    of inside and outside,
no, you delight in swallowing all sense of separation,
offer me your individuality you say,
offer up your ego mind,
offer up the waking, dream and deep sleep states!

This yoga is only for the insane
drunk on the nectar of Divine Love.
    If you drink from the Holy Grail
you will drown in the end.

The Cries Of My Beloved

I heard the cries of my Beloved
  outside my door this morning,
Throwing open the door there She stood, a little girl
  dripping the blood of violence, suffering and pain.
She entered our home to be embraced,
  washed clean with love and tears.

I heard the cries of my Beloved
  outside my door this morning,
Throwing open the door there She stood, a young woman,
  starving, deprived, tortured, battered,
  bruised, with pleading eyes.
She entered our home to be fed, nurtured, listened to and
  looked upon with loving tenderness.

I heard the cries of my Beloved
  outside my door this morning,
Throwing open the door there She was, an old woman,
  crumpled, abandoned, homeless, covered with the
  filth of human neglect.
She entered our home to be drawn out, held close and
  warmed, her life re-kindled, her gifts
  of wisdom appreciated.

Listen, listen, please listen for the cries of our Beloved.
We've been deaf for far too long.

The Wise Know

The wise know these three to be separate:
    wants, needs and Love.
By reducing their wants and needs,
    Love fills the spaciousness of their being.
They want only the end of suffering and the
    fullness of joy for all beings.
They need only that which enables them
    to fulfill their dharma.
They Love with abandon all of creation!
This is what it is to be wise.
This is what it is to be fully human.

Animals, even insects, fight over territory,
    possessions and mates, kill each other for
    food and are constantly wary of attack.
What makes you any different?
Distinguish yourself from these suffering life-forms!
You have a precious human birth,
    what are you doing with it?
Any creature can be angry, hurtful, fearful,
    and greedy.

You, you can be compassionate, loving, kind,
    patient and free.
The world cries out for your humanity, your
    wisdom, your grace.

You are Tara.
You are Kwan Yin.
You are Mary.
You are Jesus.
You are Krishna.
You are Buddha.
You are Kali.
Tat Twam Asi!
Drop your masks, drop your delusions!
Now!

Silence

All sound arises out of Silence
and dissolves into Silence.
All thought arises out of Silence
and dissolves into Silence.
The universe arises out of Silence
and dissolves into Silence.
Suffering arises out of Silence
and dissolves into Silence.
The unbounded spaciousness of Silence,
filled with the clear light of Awareness,
dissolves the roots of pain and sorrow.
Take refuge in Silence and know
unshakeable joy.

The Way To Peace

Take refuge in your breath,
Let go of the mind and rest in the breath.
Like the very dearest of friends,
Your breath has accompanied you
      through all the pains, sorrows and joys
      of your life.
Take refuge in your breath,
With loving attention follow its every movement,
Unravel the mystery of where the breath
      finds repose.

Listen with rapt attention to your dear friend,
The breath has been speaking to you
      since you were born,
Discover the mantra it whispers to you
      continuously,
Affirming the infinitude of your Being,
HAMSA is the ground on which this mad dance
      of existence pounds on....
Unravel the mystery of where mantra arises,
      and where it dissolves.

Abide in Stillness –
      the refuge of the breath,
      the source of mantra,
      the womb of all,
      where form and emptiness embrace,
      where Truth alone is revealed.
      where Love dissolves the illusion
            of differences.

(Hamsa is the ancient Sanskrit mantra that throbs with the Consciousness of
pure unbounded being and translates simply as "I AM".)

57

The One Beneath The Many

Many panes,
one light,
Many teachers,
one truth,
Many rays,
one sun,
Many rivers,
one ocean,
Many deities,
one Divine,
Many flames,
one fire,
Many sights,
one seer,
Many religions,
one Presence,
Many paths,
one summit,
Many thoughts,
one Witness,
Many forms,
one Emptiness,
Many minds,
one Awareness,
Many seekers,
One Sought,
Many lovers,
one Beloved.

Tara's Prayer

Many pains,
    one cause,
Many clouds,
    one sky,
Many egos,
    one Self,
Many struggles,
    one release,
Many shadows,
    one Light,
Many bonds,
    one freedom,
Many cloths,
    one weaver,
Many ages,
    one eternity,
Many passions,
    one Love,
Many sufferers,
    one cry for compassion,
    patience, and Love.
O Beloved Tara,
    answering the cry,
    let us serve 'til
    all are free.

If you want the ripples
on the pond to cease,
STOP SLAPPING THE WATER!

The one who thinks
"I'm meditating,"
isn't.
The One who has never thought
always is.

The greatest practice is Compassion
The greatest discipline is Patience.
The greatest path is Love.
Resolve to faithfully and enthusiastically follow these,
And you will know yourself to be Free.

Did You Know

Did you know
You can hear the hills singing,
Joined by the sky, the trees, the bushes,
The lakes and streams, the oceans and rivers,
Backed by the tiny drum beats of insects' feet,
The swoosh of millions of wings,
The sound of countless fins swaying in the water,
The pounding of the waves and the
rustling song of the stones
Stirred in joy by the surf!

Listen, listen for God singing
His songs of Love to Himself!

Become still, listen......
The stars are singing to you!
The earth, the moon and all the planets
have joined in the chorus!

Your breath is singing,
your friends are singing, your enemies are singing – listen,
please listen and you'll hear!

*Shivo'ham, Shivo'ham, Chidananda Rupaha
Shivo'ham Shivo'ham!*

Analhaq! Analhaq! Analhaq! Analhaq!

*Aham Brahm'asmi! Aham Brahm'asmi!
Aham Brahm'asmi!*

Hamsa! Hamsa! Hamsa! Hamsa!

*I am Shiva, I am the Auspicious One, I am the form of
Consciousness and Bliss,
I am Shiva, I am Shiva!*

I am Allah! I am Allah! I am Allah! I am Allah!

*I am Brahman! I am Brahman! I am Brahman!
I am Brahman!*

*I am That! I am That! I am That!
I am That!*

YOU, you are all that!
You are the hills, the mountains, the rivers, the oceans,
You are all the creatures and all the people
and all creation!

*You are God singing your songs of Love to Yourself!
Without you the song would be incomplete.
Without all of creation the song would be incomplete.
Preserve it all, every creature, every being,
Keep your song of songs full and true.
Know that your Divine Love embraces all.*

Choose Love

If you take what the Buddha and Christ said,
and all the great yogis, saints, sages,
mystics, and lovers of God,
it can be reduced to two words:
Choose Love.
There is nothing higher than Love,
nothing purer,
nothing more selfless,
nothing more powerful,
and it is present in every moment.
Choose Love.
In all times, in all places -
Choose Love,
for Love has already chosen you.

HAMSA

My Dear One,
You've sought to see me
as you wanted to see me.

You've sought to hold me
as you wanted to hold me.

You've caught glimpses of your Beloved
and your eyes filled with tears of joy,
washing away the suffering of the world.

You've felt the brush of my Holy Spirit
and delighted in the ecstasy
that blossomed in your body.

My Dear One,
It is time to
surrender.

Surrender seeking to see me
as you want to see me.

Surrender seeking to hold me
as you want to hold me.

It is time to behold me as

I Am.

Shambhala

Love's touch
stripped by fear
of Love's grace
leaves withered bodies
like logs for the funeral pyre
consuming the Heart's
true wishes.
All that remains
are dust and ash.

The ceaseless winds of
Love's relentless Spirit
breathe life renewing
strength into aging matter
blowing fear away forever.

Delight in the fearless
Spaciousness of Freedom.

Shambhala is your true home.

The Knower

Darkness is secondary.
> Who is the Knower
>> Who illumines all darkness?

Light is secondary.
> Who is the Knower
>> Who illumines even the sun?

Mystery is secondary.
> Who is the Knower
>> Who penetrates all mysteries?

Knowledge is secondary.
> Who is the Knower
>> Who is the source of all knowledge?

Wisdom is secondary.
> Who is the Knower
>> The Wellspring of wisdom
>> From whom all scriptures have come?

Pleasure and suffering are secondary.
> Who is the Knower,
>> The stainless One untouched by
>> desire and attachment,
>> who looks upon all with love and
>>> compassion?

Form and emptiness are secondary.
> Who is the Knower
>> In whose clear and boundless
>> Light of awareness
>> Form and emptiness embrace?

Birth and death are secondary.
> Who is the Knower
>> The One, Unborn,
>> Undying, Eternally Pure?

O my Beloved,
> *Tat Tvam Asi!*
> *Thou art That!*

O beloved Rinpoche
you gave your life
as a mirror to the world
reflecting its drunken
madness – suffering,
addicted to emptiness it is,
illusion,
while living in
the Buddhafield of
     spacious awareness.

You cut through
     myths of freedom
     and spiritual materialism,
illuminating the grasping,
     craving mind.

O Trungpa Rinpoche,
how the earth misses
the gentle touch
of your lotus feet.

Let your mind return to its original nature as Mind
Everything else will find its rightful place
And assume its rightful size in your life.
This boundless Mind embraces all,
This boundless Mind is boundless Heart.
Know this and know the Love that embraces All.

Snow and rain
blow through the sky
like thoughts and feelings
through the mind.
Have you seen the face
of the one who makes the weather?
The powerful illusion of a thinker
Seduces all but those
Who have traversed the Way.

Even the high priests
    of science, the physicists,
in their relentless pursuit of Mistress Sophia,
    unwittingly
have found their way to the outer precincts
of your mysteries,
my beloved Kali.

They pronounce
that if one adds up
all the energy available
plus all the atoms
in all the planets
plus all the billions and billions of stars
in all the galaxies
in all the universe
you only get 5%
of all that is!!!!

How can this be???
What makes up the rest of all that is????

The high priests of science, the physicists
    have an answer –
dark matter and dark energy!

O my beloved Kali,
    are you playing with them
as they go sniffing around
    black holes?

If they only knew the intoxicating scent
    of your sweet yoni,
they would know what is truly
    worth seeking!

Your bindu,
womb and tomb,
portal between the finite and the infinite,
Shri Bindu,
known to Tilopa and Naropa,
mystery of mysteries,
summoning true lovers of Sophia
to the darkness beyond darkness.

Gaté Gaté Paragaté Parasamgaté Bodhi Swaha!

Waiting in a crowded airport
watching as a mother,
sitting with her infant,
placed the child on the floor between her feet,
while the child happily played
with a toy in his lap.

Suddenly he looked up;
seeing all the strangers,
fear and pain stole the joy from his face,
letting out a cry and starting to flail his arms,
he caught his mothers attention.

She merely wiggled her feet,
touched his shoulder,
and he collapsed back against her legs.
Happily squirming up against those
reassuring pillars,
he let out a laugh as his mother began
playing hide and seek with him.

You are the Divine
Sitting in the lap of the Divine
caught up in playing with the mind,
a magnificent toy, not doubt,
but you're taking it far too seriously!
You're worse than an x-box addict!

Wake up!
Stop playing with yourself
long enough to remember who
you truly are and where you sit!
It's time to laugh
and play with true freedom!

O my Beloved
   where are you?

Midnight has come and gone,
   1 o'clock, 1:30, 2...
   Where are you?

At last I feel your
   approach, my Beloved!

There, the liquid sounds of
   your robes coming down
   the hallways to my chamber.

I peek out and see the
   velvet black hem of
   your raiment as you turn
   the last corner and
   approach me.

Why have you made me wait so long?

"Longing and waiting,
   prepare and purify, my Dear One."

Remember before we met
   and I was so afraid of you?

Even when the Teacher brought me
   into your presence,
   I couldn't look at you, my Beloved.

When You finally drew my gaze into yours,
    suddenly I knew
    there never was
    a time we didn't know
    and love each other.

But your mysterious,
    impenetrable darkness
    still frightened me, my Beloved!

How silly it seems now
    as I run to your velvet black embrace,
Diving into your mysteries that only pure
Love illuminates,
    and leaves intact.

Poor mind, extinguished by your
sweet and gentle breath,
    unable to enter the infinite spaciousness
    where two become
    One.

One clear Light.
One boundless Joy.
One eternal, all-embracing
    Love.

O Dear Mother
You are Spanda,
The throb of the Infinite
Giving name and form to the Absolute,
Your Beloved Spouse.
You pulsate as maha-mantra,
Freeing us from the snares of your little mothers,
Whose words and thoughts
create the limited mind and all it suffers.
May we take refuge in your holy name,
the vehicle of mantra
Which unfailingly dissolves the many
Into One.

Caught Unawares

My Beloved caught me
    unawares today.

I hurried home from work,
    pulled in our driveway,
    my mind sorting its daily 'to do' list,
    complaining to itself about the
    number of unfinished items and
    the scarcity of time.

While opening the car door a zephyr caressed
    my face and delivered a scent
    so sublime it arrested my mind,
    demanding that it be followed
    back to its source.

There in the garden above,
    an exquisite white lily blossomed,
    Her beauty and fragrance filling the yard,
    Her swollen buds promising even more.

Standing in Her presence
    a portal opened to the domain of the eternal
    and a tear of joy slid down my cheek.

Her summons to remember had been answered.

Cars continued to rush by on the road
    not twenty feet away,
    the sounds of children playing at the beach
    drifted across the lake,
    a cat bird flitted from branch to branch on the
    crabapple tree nearby, looking at us standing there.
    Was he too drawn close by Her presence?

Time and space are Her gifts,
    as suffused with Her presence as is the air
    with the lily's intoxicating scent.

She so generously sprinkles throughout space and time
    Her calls to awaken and remember.

My Beloved, you take special delight in tripping the mind
    and watching it fall into your ocean of ecstasy!

O my Beloved,
what will you become
when you are through
becoming me?

Infinite waves arise
and subside,
the Infinite ocean
of your sweet Being,
delighting
in every form You take,
and in turn,
dissolving each
in Your loving embrace.

All cravings are but
one longing
for the sublime joy
of coming to rest in You.
By your grace
all the streams and rivers
of our desires,
set in motion by You,
flow irresistibly into You.

Who can know Your delight,
without becoming You?

Blaring horn in the middle
of the night,
Resistance gives way to
awakening.

I keep searching for wisdom
      only to dissolve in ecstasy!
What's the ordinary mind to do?

Surrender to the rapturous
      singing and dancing
Of Lover and Beloved!

The mind conjures an end
little knowing
that even its beginning
was imagined.

The one you love
the one you miss -
the world's a mirror
for you to kiss!

Is there no end
    to the suffering
Inflicted by an
    undisciplined mind?

Meditate Kalidas.
Know true freedom
    and true peace.
Quench the fires
    of the mind.

As illusory as they may be
    they scorch the three worlds.

As a child I learned
      of the great continents like isles on the five world oceans,
each so vast that huge ships a quarter mile long
      disappear on their surface like specks of dust.

What a mystery to discover countless other oceans,
      each dwarfing all seas combined.
So overwhelmingly immeasurable they are
      that no shore will you find.

Where, where are these mysterious oceans?
      Look in the eyes of any being,
         truly look and you will see
oceans of love, seas of compassion, waves of
      glorious consciousness rising and falling,
         sparkling and radiant...

    O how can I ever tear my eyes from yours my dear?

What a veil you
hide behind, my Beloved!

This shroud of thoughts and words
appears impenetrable

until touched
by your sweet love!

Threads set aquiver...
what sublime ecstasy
is this divine unraveling!

One morning my beloved Devi whispered:

"All minds are mine,
No mind is me."

A few days later She whispered:

"Every body is my body,
No body is me.

Every form is my form,
No form is me.

O, but it is such fun to pretend!"

O Matrika Shaktis,
little mothers,
you've done your work

concealing the
inconceivable

like the child
of a barren woman.

Now use your power
to reveal
the never hidden.

It's All About Stillness

It's all about stillness,
this life,
this death,
this moment arising,
this moment swallowed
by Kali Ma.

The ever-present Stillness of Being,
Infinite, Spacious, Eternally Free,
Kali's Beloved,
Lord Shiva,
You and me.

Move with that Awareness throughout the day,
through periods of silence, meditation, and chanting,
through walking, eating, speaking, and working.
All movement arises out of stillness.
Return to stillness over and over and over...

Watch the mind.
See how it craves movement,
how it begs attention to follow its
    desires and attachments.
See how letting go of these
    immediately opens the experience of spaciousness,
    of bare Awareness,
the distant movements of thoughts and perceptions
    darting about like fireflies in the night sky.

Every moment my Dear One
is an opportunity to look beyond
    the movements of mind
which delude you into feeling
you are that tiny, ephemeral, collection of fireflies!

Know the Infinite expanse of the Sky of Awareness.
Become a Sky Dancer!
Know you are Shiva!
You are Buddha!

Om Tat Sat

True Hope
the divine scent of wisdom's blossoms,
Beckons you to follow the Way,
your sure path beyond all suffering.

True Hope,
the footprints of Buddhas and bodhisattvas,
still warm from their passing,
infuses your step with enthusiasm and certainty.
Dash ahead, right now!
Go from
I can be free
to
I am free,
from
We all can be free
to
We all are free!
Emaho!

Now!
The End is Now.
The Beginning Is Now.
Bring all your attention to this point.
All your attention. NOW.

My dear One,
Everyone enjoys being loved.
All beings delight in love coursing
    through them.
All want to be happy.
All want to enjoy good health and a long life.
All are loving sons and daughters
    rising from the same Source.

Can you harm a son or daughter
    without piercing the Mother and Father?

In this moment do you choose
    to love all sons and daughters?
Are you cultivating the sweet fruit of
    compassion and kindness for every being?
That sublime nectar can be yours right now!

Enough of bitterness, anger and revenge.
What has cultivating these brought to anyone
    but agony
    to mothers and fathers,
    sons and daughters.

Even if it is just for your own pleasure,
    choose the boundless joy of living with
    compassion and kindness for all.

Choose.
Now.

Teach the Will
the ego-mind's drive,
to surrender gently to the Divine,
like a snowflake falling,
silently settling,
its destined place in the field of snow
embracing its perfection.

The One who knows, knows all this
and delights in the life-course of every snowflake,
every living creature, every thing.

Letting go and letting go and letting go...
Freedom is already fully present.
Letting go and letting go and letting go...
Of illusion, pain and suffering.

Letting go and letting go and letting go...
Fall onto the exquisitely soft bed of Love
She has waiting for you!

Kali's Bazaar

This is where your every
    footstep lands,
Look around,
    for Kali all things are possible.

In Kali's Bazaar
    the infinite becomes finite
And emptiness
    parades as form.

In Kali's Bazaar,
    those born of love
    kill in hatred,
blind to their delusions,
    flailing about in self-inflicted agony,
destroying others
    instead of their own ignorance.

In Kali's Bazaar,
    where the most loving, kind, and compassionate monks
    are silently tortured and murdered by deluded
    Chinese soldiers,
where countless children, mothers and fathers
    starve to death,
    their cries of hunger unheard,
while people spend incalculable billions to watch a ball hit,
    kicked, thrown or bounced to make a
    quickly forgotten score.

In Kali's Bazaar
    where your craving for reflections of yourself
has led you into a hall where thousands of mirror shards
    give you glimpses
    of what you frantically seek.

In Kali's Bazaar
    your karma has deposited you.
Peer through the darkness,
    you will see buddhas and bodhisattvas,
    sages and saints,
Lao Tzu, Christ, Tara, Krishna, Mary and Kwan Yin,
    all actors in this final act of Kali Ma's 4 act play.
Follow their light,
    marking Her graceful paths to freedom.
No need to hurry if you like the show,
No need to worry if you slept through the earlier acts,
    this play repeats itself forever within
Kali's Bazaar, the realm of time.

When you finally tire of becoming
    the victim and the perpetrator,
    the hunter and the hunted,
    the hunger and the food,
    the embraced and the rejected,
    the sinner and the saint,
    the bound and the free
    the seeker and the sought,
    the shadow and the light,
it's simply time to wake up!

We humans are so like pigs
    you can pluck a valve
from a pig's heart and implant it
    into a person
and it works fine! (for the human)

Who said the One who has created
    this All
doesn't have a sense of humor?

She's still laughing!
She understands,
    having been worshipped for countless centuries
    as a great sow.

Of course She finds even greater delight
    when we cultivate our immeasurable capacities
    for love, compassion and patience,
that distinguish us from swine.

You lovingly, enthusiastically
sacrificed all
for I to exist.

And some count as a sign
of God's generosity
that He gave a Son.
Sadly they couldn't see
past one.

You know the infinite
sons and daughters you've born,
and the infinite yet to come.

Years ago you sent brother pain
    and sister agony
To teach me lessons not yet learned
    from brother anger and sister impatience.
Not that they had left!
You just added to the teaching staff!
You are so very generous!

Winter Sun Falling On Closed Eyes
    warm orange glow filling my sight.
The shadow of a bird
    passing in flight,
Streaking over my eyelids
    gone before the mind could name it,
Yet, the joy lingers on
    in simple delight.

Loyal Companions
    body and mind,
Bear burdens serving
    with joy
The Divine.

High on a ledge
   in the temple
sparrows happily twitter and mate.

They know this joyous act of worship.
   Why not the somber monks below?

Dear old body
    fiery pain prolongs the night
Chandrika pours moon beams
    to cool the way.
Om Namah Chandrika

There are those who advocate
    the pursuits and pleasures of the ordinary mind;
the eyes-open, waking state
    is all-valuable they find.

For others asleep to the allures
    of sense pleasures,
it's the super-sensuous domain
    they treasure.

Transcendent love and Divine Presence
    outshine the mind's borrowed light,
leaving it as blind as common vision
    in the dark of night.

Ahh, but to keep the company of those
    rare beings
for whom eyes open or closed, awake or asleep
    blind or seeing
no longer have the slightest meaning,
this is the way, the path,
    to freedom everlasting.

Cherishing yourself
    you cherish your opinions.
You have an opinion even about your opinions!
But you don't stop there,
    you have an opinion about your opinion
        of opinions!

How long before you realize
    you are chasing your tail?
Where do you think the stench of the world
    comes from?

Transcend the world
    and you're just a gasbag.
Live gripped by the world
    and you're just a dirtbag.

The Way is neither here nor there.
Not one, not two.

Give up thinking about it.
Thought goes no farther
    than steam rising from your tea.

Give up trying to meditate.
Cease all movements to and fro.

Your essence is the Way,
    look no further.

A moment has yet to pass
    when you weren't All.

After all

After all words have been spoken,
After all dharmas have been completed,
After all mantras have been chanted,
After all visions have ceased,
Spacious awareness,
Silent and free
remains.

Shiva, Shiva Mahadeva
Namah Shivayah Sadashiva
What use have I for calling out
My own Name
When it is my Beloved Kali
I eternally long for!
Kali! Kali! Kali! Kali!
Ma Kali Mahadevi!
How you delight in putting on
the form of the universe and
doing your love dance for me to watch!
There's not one of your forms that doesn't know
the warm caress of my adoring lips.

This is it my Friend!
This day is it!
This day is the unfolding
    of the Glory of God!

This is it my Friend!
This hour is it!
This hour is the unfolding
    of the Glory of God!

This is it my Friend!
This moment is it!
This moment is the unfolding
    of the Glory of God!

This is it my Friend!
This breath is it!
This breath is the unfolding
    of the Glory of God!

This is it my Friend!
This creation is it!
This creation is the unfolding
    of the Glory of God!

(The Devi visited me with this poem as sat stuck in rush hour traffic on my way to work at the hospital one morning, neuropathic pain firing through my back and leg, just days before having back surgery to free pinched nerves. There is no time, no place where Her Glory isn't continuously present.)

When love
meets Love
no words
are uttered,

like pools
of water
merging
in silence,

they
become
One.

Shed your clothes my Dear
  stand naked in the Light!

Shed your thoughts
  like clothes, they block
    the Light.

Stand naked in the
  blazing Light.

Shed any thought of It
  as a Being,
even this vain attempt of the mind
to grasp the ungraspable dissolves.

Stand naked in the
  hurricane of Light!
Whirling cascades of
  of radiant Love at last
    erasing the barest
      wisp of you.

What fun!

O my Beloved
what fun
pretending there's a We
when we both know
there isn't even a
me!

I went to the Master
simply to be free.
She opened my heart,
tore off the veil,
leaving no bonds
holding anything to
this phantom me.

Now this puppet
dances on.
Who holds
the strings?

Mother of Time
Devourer of Now
She delights
in playing
the I
She wanted
me to be.

O My Beloved
no matter how you
you hide your beauty,
no matter how many
cloaks you wear,
no matter how far
beneath layers
of evil.
of pain,
of disease,
of misfortune
of disaster,
of lack,
of greed,
of ignorance,
of riches,
of banality,
of delight,
of longing,
of beauty,
of allure,
of beliefs,
of concepts,
of myths,
of darkness,
of light,
of time,
of space,
of matter,
of mystery,
your lovers see you
issuing them all
from your
unfathomable Womb.

The flute
has but
one job:
to remain open.
And even that
is accomplished
by its creator.

May Maha Kali
reveal Her sweet face
in all that you encounter,
in all that you taste,
in all that you seek,
in all that you cherish,
and all that you love,
no matter how quickly
these will perish.

May you know Her grace
in all times and every place.

The tides of your breath
are your constant reminder
that She infuses your body
with Her life and power.
Your every inhalation is Her exhalation.
Your every exhalation is Her inhalation.
Remember this and you will live
and die in Grace.

Other Books by Lawrence Edwards, PhD

The Soul's Journey: Guidance From The Divine Within
(2000, iUniverse)

Kundalini Rising: Exploring the Energy of Awakening
(Contributing Author, 2009, Sounds True, Inc.)

Available in bookstores and Amazon.com

OTHER HELPFUL BOOKS BY
THE WHITFIELDS

Dr. Whitfield explains in some detail how the reader can use practical and proven non-drug techniques and recovery aids. Caution: This book contains an indictment of the psychiatric drug industry and an enlightening exposure of their dogma for the people who are taking these brain disabling drugs and those who care for them.

—Peter R. Breggin, MD, Psychiatrist and author of *Medication Madness*

This is not an easy book to read. It contains real-life pain, sadness and loss. Some of us have suffered like Carole did --and worse-- yet in reading this book — we discover healing. There is help here. And most importantly, there is hope within these pages for anyone who has been severely and repeatedly traumatized, abused and/or neglected in childhood. Whitfield quotes from Carole's documentary: "The thunderstorms are just as beautiful as a sunny day. And so is life!"

—Donald Brennan from the Foreword

OTHER HELPFUL BOOKS BY
THE WHITFIELDS

This book is a continuation of Volume I, Choosing God: A Bird's Eye View of A Course in Miracles -- of this two volume pair.

In this book I pick up where the first book ended. Here I summarize 15 more key Course topics plus a new original chapter, The Universal Message of the Course in which I compare the Course to world religions and spiritual paths, including Alcoholics Anonymous and other Twelve Step Fellowships.

"Charles takes us into the heart and soul of A Course in Miracles"

**Jyoti and Russell Park, PhD
Center for Sacred Studies**

Teachers of God

Further Reflections on
A Course in Miracles

Charles L. Whitfield, MD
Author of Healing The Child Within
and
The Power of Humility

ṁ ḣ ṗ
muse house press

"So much has been written and said about the soul. In this book, we are shown the soul. Whitfield illustrated how to live from our soul and relate to the souls of others.

I have come to regard this book as a postcard from Whitfield's soul to ours, and my advice is to read it, say "thank you," and put it into practice."

**Bruce Greyson, M.D.,
Chester F. Carlson Professor of Psychiatry and Neurobehavioral Sciences, University of Virginia School of Medicine**

Foreword by Charles L. Whitfield, M.D.

SPIRITUAL AWAKENINGS

INSIGHTS OF THE NEAR-DEATH EXPERIENCE AND OTHER DOORWAYS TO OUR SOUL

Barbara Harris Whitfield

More Books by Our Authors

Barbara is a gifted
writer with the ability
to take on the complex
subject of the Soul. As
a Near Death
Experience myself, her
insight coupled with
compassion, wit and
humor helped me to a
greater understanding
of my Inner Self and
how to connect with
my Soul.
—Sharon Cormier
500 RYT Yoga Teacher

**Coming 2012
from
Charles Whitfield MD**

MuseHousePress.com